Kingfishers to Bullet Trains

Tech from Nature

By Jennifer Colby

21st Century
Junior Library

Published in the United States of America by
Cherry Lake Publishing
Ann Arbor, Michigan
www.cherrylakepublishing.com

Reading Adviser: Marla Conn, MS, Ed., Literacy specialist, Read-Ability, Inc.
Content Adviser: Rachel Brown, MA, Sustainable Business

Photo Credits: © NaturesMomentsuk/Shutterstock.com, Cover, 1 [left]; © kawamura_lucy/Shutterstock.com, Cover, 1 [right]; © FeelGoodLuck/Shutterstock.com, 4; © Ken Cole/Dreamstime, 6; © Wangkun Jia/Dreamstime, 8; © Phuong D. Nguyen/Shutterstock.com, 10; © David734240/Dreamstime, 12; © Sean Pavone/Dreamstime, 14; © Michal Ninger/Shutterstock.com, 16; © Azman Salleh/Shutterstock.com, 18; © Banky405/Dreamstime, 20

Copyright ©2019 by Cherry Lake Publishing. All rights reserved. No part of this book may be reproduced or utilized in any form or by any means without written permission from the publisher.

Library of Congress Cataloging-in-Publication Data

Names: Colby, Jennifer, 1971– author.
Title: Kingfishers to bullet trains / Jennifer Colby.
Description: Ann Arbor : Cherry Lake Publishing, [2019] | Series: Tech from nature | Audience: Grade 4 to 6. | Includes bibliographical references and index.
Identifiers: LCCN 2018035195 | ISBN 9781534142930 (hardcover) | ISBN 9781534140691 (pdf) | ISBN 9781534139497 (pbk.) | ISBN 9781534141896 (hosted ebook)
Subjects: LCSH: High speed trains—Juvenile literature. | Birds—Flight—Juvenile literature. | Noise control—Juvenile literature. | Biomimicry—Juvenile literature.
Classification: LCC TF1455 .C65 2019 | DDC 625.2—dc23
LC record available at https://lccn.loc.gov/2018035195

Cherry Lake Publishing would like to acknowledge the work of the Partnership for 21st Century Skills. Please visit *www.p21.org* for more information.

Printed in the United States of America
Corporate Graphics

CONTENTS

5 Fast and Safe

7 Speeding Through History

11 Hey, Turn That Down!

17 Investigating Nature

22 Glossary
23 Find Out More
24 Index
24 About the Author

Train travel can be faster than cars.

Fast and Safe

Have you ever watched a train go by? It's fast! Over time, travel by train has improved.

Steam locomotives are still used in some places.

Speeding Through History

Railroads have been around for thousands of years. The earliest **railways** were in ancient Greece. Wagons were pulled through **grooves** in the road.

The first steam-powered **locomotive** was developed in the early 1800s in England. Wood or coal was burned to create the steam that moved the **pistons**. These controlled the train's wheels.

Diesel locomotives are used to pull trains carrying passengers and goods.

Germany was the first to power its trains with electricity. It was used in combination with **diesel fuel** to power locomotives. That was in the early 1900s. In 1964, the bullet train was introduced in Japan. Traveling by train was forever changed!

Look!

Find different types of locomotives. Use the internet or your library to compare the different types.

The bullet train changed the way people travel in Japan.

Hey, Turn That Down!

Japanese "bullet trains" are nicknamed for their shape and speed. They can reach speeds of 200 miles (322 kilometers) per hour!

The trains only run on electricity. They are better for the environment than other types of trains. But up until the 1990s, they had a big problem. The bullet train made too much noise when traveling from place to place.

Pantographs connect electric trains to power lines.

One way the train made too much noise was through its power source. An **antenna** sits on top of each train car. These antennas are called **pantographs**.

The air blowing over the pantographs made a lot of noise. The Japanese government has strict rules on **noise pollution**. They do not want people to be bothered.

Another noise-related problem involved mountain tunnels. The bullet trains traveled faster than the speed of sound. Every time a train passed through a tunnel, it created a **sonic boom**.

Bullet train routes are planned to avoid heavily populated areas.

The Japanese government asked a team of **engineers** to solve these noise issues. The team was led by Eiji Nakatsu. But Nakatsu wasn't only an engineer. He was also a bird-watcher.

Make a Guess!

Can you guess what other countries have bullet trains? Write down your guess. Then ask an adult to help you find the answer.

Owls provided the answer to the problem of noisy pantographs.

Investigating Nature

Engineers had used the knowledge of birds' bodies and how they flew to create airplanes. Nakatsu thought that the noise problems could be solved through the study of birds.

An owl swoops down and grabs its prey in almost total silence. Tiny, **sawtooth**-shaped feathers silence the swirling air around the owl's wings. Engineers added strips of wing-shaped metal with **notched** edges to the

The study of a small bird called the kingfisher solved another sound problem.

pantographs. Their idea was based on the concept of **biomimicry**. This reduced the train's noise.

Next was the problem of sonic booms. Nakatsu thought a sudden change in **air pressure** was the problem. He believed the train experienced this when it traveled through tunnels.

One day, he saw the kingfisher bird. He watched it swoop down to break through the surface of the water. That was how it caught

Create!

Different birds have different wing shapes. These differences affect how they fly. You can test this out yourself! Make paper airplanes with different wing designs to see how they fly. Do some designs swoop? Do others fly a longer distance?

The nose design makes bullet trains quieter.

its prey. The bird made very little noise and barely even splashed! Nakatsu determined this was because of the kingfisher's long and slender beak.

The team redesigned the nose of the bullet train to look like the kingfisher's beak. The issues with the sonic booms were fixed.

The study of birds has been very useful. Their special **anatomy** is copied for the design of today's bullet trains. Now bullet trains are here to stay.

Ask Questions!

Ask your friends and family about the different types of transportation they have used. Can they be improved? Look to nature for inspiration to help improve their design!

GLOSSARY

air pressure (AIR presh-ur) the force of air on any surface in contact with it

anatomy (uh-NAT-uh-mee) the parts that form a living thing

antenna (an-TEN-uh) a device (such as a wire or a metal rod) for moving electricity

biomimicry (bye-oh-MIM-ik-ree) copying plants and animals to build or improve something

diesel fuel (DEE-zuhl FYOO-uhl) a type of fuel that is sometimes used in large vehicles

engineers (en-juh-NEERZ) people trained to design and build machines such as trains

grooves (GROOVZ) long, narrow cuts in the surface of something hard

locomotive (loh-kuh-MOH-tiv) the vehicle that produces the power that pulls a train

noise pollution (NOIZ puh-LOO-shuhn) loud or unpleasant noise that is harmful or annoying to the people who can hear it

notched (NAHCHT) a cut in the shape of a V in an edge or surface

pantographs (PAN-tuh-grafs) antennas moving current to a train from overhead wires

pistons (PIS-tuhnz) parts of an engine that move up and down inside a tube and that cause other parts of the engine to move

railways (RAYL-wayz) a system of tracks on which trains travel

sawtooth (SAW-tooth) having sharp edges like those of a saw

sonic boom (SAH-nik BOOM) the loud noise made by a vehicle when it goes faster than the sound waves it produces

FIND OUT MORE

BOOKS

Togo, Narisa. *Magnificent Birds*. Somerville, MA: Candlewick Press, 2018.

Wood, John. *Travel Technology: Maglev Trains, Hovercrafts, and More.* New York: Gareth Stevens Publishing, 2018.

WEBSITES

Cornell Lab of Ornithology—All About Birds: Belted Kingfisher
https://www.allaboutbirds.org/guide/Belted_Kingfisher/overview
Learn about kingfishers' habitat, location, and sounds, as well as how to identify them in the wild.

DK Find Out!—Transport
https://www.dkfindout.com/uk/transport
This website explains the history of aircraft, cars, tractors, and trains. Take an online quiz to see what you have learned.

INDEX

A
air pressure, 19

B
beak, 21
biomimicry, 19
birds, 15, 17, 18
bullet train, 9, 10, 14
    noise, 11, 13, 19, 20
    nose of, 20, 21

E
electricity, 9, 11, 12

F
feathers, 17

J
Japan, 9, 10, 11

K
kingfishers, 18, 19, 21

L
locomotives, 6, 7, 8, 9

N
Nakatsu, Eiji, 15, 17, 21
noise, 11, 13, 17, 18

O
owls, 16, 17

P
pantographs, 12, 13, 16, 17

S
sonic boom, 13, 19, 21
speed of sound, 13

T
trains, 4, 5, 7, 8. *See also* bullet train
tunnels, 13, 19

ABOUT THE AUTHOR

Jennifer Colby is a school librarian in Ann Arbor, Michigan. She loves reading, traveling, and going to museums to learn about new things.